~Introducing Fiqh Series~
Vol.4

Introducing the Fiqh of Zakat
(فقه الزكاة)

Written and compiled by

SAFARUK Z. CHOWDHURY

AD-DUHA
LONDON 2009

First edition 2009

Updated Edition 2009

An educational publication from Ad-Duha London
Third Floor, 42 Fieldgate Street
London E1 1ES
E: info@duha.org.uk
W: www.duha.org.uk
T: 07891 421 925

3

Contents Page

Section:	Page
Table of Contents	5
Table of Symbols	5
§1. Introduction	6-8
§2. Preliminaries	9
Chapter 1: §3. Basic definitions:	10-19

- Zakat (زكاة).
- Nisab (نصاب).
- *Faqir / Miskin* (فقير، مسكين)

Chapter 2: §4. Conditions pertaining to Zakat	20-24

- One lunar year.
- Intention.

Chapter 3:	25-26

- §5. Key Zakat Recipients

- §6. Non-Zakat Recipients

Chapter 4: §7. Non-Zakat Areas	27-29
Chapter 5: §8. Zakat and the State	30

4

TABLE OF ABBREVIATIONS

Art.   = article

Bk.   = book

pp.   = pages

`   = the Arabic letter ع

'   = the Arabic letter ء

اهـ.   = 'end of quote' where a cited textual segment in Arabic ends.

s: = additional comments made by the translator

Table of Symbols

\#   = *hadith* number

(…)   = contains transliteration of Arabic terms

[…]   = contains additions by the translator

… / […]   = ellipsis where a textual segment is elided and omitted in translation by the translator

{…}   = enclosure of a Qur'anic verse in translation

§   = section

INTRODUCING THE *FIQH* OF *ZAKAT*

الحمد لله حمداً يبلغ رضاه وصلى الله على أشرف من اجتباه
وعلى من صاحبه ووالاه وسلم تسليماً لا يدرك منتهاه.

Praise be to Allah Most High; The Giver of this perfect and final Law for all times and abundant blessings upon our beloved Prophet, the Divine Mercy sent for humankind who embodied this perfect Law and implemented it for all to follow and who is the Light of Guidance that has radiated the firmaments. Blessings too upon his noble Companions who followed His blessed example in implementing this sacred Law, his pure family and all those who follow them in creed and deed until the Final Day. To proceed:

♦

§1. Introduction

1. Our law is sacred because it is From Allah (swt).[1]
2. Our Sacred Law is the most perfect legal system because it is from Allah (swt).[2]

---

[1] Shah `Abd al-Haqq al-Dihlawi, *Takmil al-Iman*, p.101.
[2] Shah `Abd al-Haqq al-Dihlawi, *Takmil al-Iman*, p.101.

3. Our Sacred Law has abrogated all previous legal systems and indeed our *din* has abrogated all earlier religions.[3]

- It is the view of all *usuli* scholars as well as theologians that the human mind (*'aql*) cannot ascertain what is right and what is wrong related to moral actions and indeed any action.[4]

- It is also the view of the *usuli* scholars that legal injunctions and rulings pertaining to food and drinks may often elude rational evaluations and so the believer takes these on the utter conviction and trust that the Lawgiver – Allah (swt) – has legislated them in the general best interest of human beings and that there is wisdom (*hikam*) underpinning them.

- The same point extends to humanity's greatest blessing (and indeed that of all creation) the beloved of Allah our beloved the Messenger of Allah (may the abundant peace and blessings of Allah be upon him) and his pure and blessed *sunna* (example).

- Hence, our immediate consternation of being unable to determine any sense or coherence upon coming to know the relevant legal injunctions and rulings does not warrant the inference that they neither have coherence nor are they practically enforceable. *We listen and we obey.*

---

[3] Shah 'Abd al-Haqq al-Dihlawi, *Takmil al-Iman*, p.147.
[4] al-Nabhani, *al-Shakhsiyya al-Islamiyya*, 3:14-18.

- It is also our conviction that our legal tradition has been delineated by the greatest legal minds and personalities unrivalled in any civilisation.

- We believe that our noble scholar-jurists (*mujtahidun* and *fuqaha'*) were:

  1. Trustworthy.
  2. Qualified.
  3. Pious.
  4. Sincere.
  5. But fallible.

- Moreover, we approach the study of the *fiqh* with humility and reverence but with a critical engagement of this legacy. And may Allah enable us to carry out the tasks required of us. *Amin.*

- This is a small booklet outlining some very basic legal injunctions and rulings pertaining to Zakat as expounded within the School (*madhhab*) of the noble Imam Abu Hanifa Nu`man b. Thabit (80-150/768) – may Allah be pleased with him. There is no extensive analysis nor are their comparative discussions and evaluations although some *fiqh* discussions are given of some common questions surrounding zakat and its fulfilment with regard to contemporary issues. Although primarily written for class format, It is hoped that this small contribution helps those who read it and nothing is asked of them except sincere *du`as.*[5]

---

[5] No evidential discussions are presented in the booklet for lack of space and due to the requirement of pre-requisite knowledge of *usul al-fiqh.*

§2. Preliminaries

- Zakat is one of the foundational pillars of Islam.[6]

- Zakat is obligatory and so must be discharged.[7]

- Deliberately avoiding zakat is a major sin and denial of it is disbelief.

- The *fada'il* ('excellences'/'merits') and reward associated with it are mentioned in innumerable books by our righteous scholars and does not form the material of this booklet.[8]

For Hanafi textual evidences, see al-Bahlawi, *Adillat al-Hanafiyya*, pp.289-330. For detailed accounts of Hanafi rulings, refer to *al-Hidaya*, 1:103-126 (= English translation, 1:245-302); al-Nasafi, *Kanz al-Daqa'iq*, pp.22-25; al-Quduri, *Mukhtasar*, pp. (= al-Ghunaymi's *al-Lubab*, 1:136-153) and S. al-Nadwi, *al-Fiqh al-Muyassar*, pp.203-215. For basic comparative assessments between *madhhabs*, consult al-al-Jaziri, *Fiqh ʿAla al-Madhahib al-Arbaʿa* (English translation by N. Roberts), 1:795-892.

[6] Alahazrat Imam Ahmad Reza Khan, *Aʿazz al-Iktinah*, pp.174-175.

[7] Alahazrat, *Aʿazz al-Iktina*, p.173.

[8] Alahazrat, *Aʿazz al-Iktina*, pp.172-178.

CHAPTER ONE

§3. Basic Definitions

- Below are explanations of the words 'Zakat', 'Nisab' and 'Faqir/Miskin':

[1] *Zakat* **('almsgiving'):** variously translated as 'alms', 'poor tax', 'charity tax', 'wealth tax' and 'tax' although it is not a tax in the strict sense.[9] Below is a legal definition of "*zakat*" from *Tanwir al-Absar* of Imam al-Tumurtashi:

هي تمليك جزء مال عينه الشارع من مسلم فقير غير هاشمي ولا مولاه مع قطع المنفعة عن المملك من كل وجه لله تعالى

"It is [s: defined as] transferring ownership of a part of one's wealth specified by the Lawgiver to a poor and needy Muslim who is not a Hashimi or their client without any benefits accrued from the giver all exclusively for the sake of Allah Most high..."[10]

---

[9] There are two linguistic meanings to the word "*zakat*": [1] purity (*al-tahara*) as in Q. 9:103 and [2] growth and increase (*al-ziyada*). See al-Shurunbulali, *Nur al-Idah*, p.345.

[10] Ibn `Abidin, *Radd al-Muhtar*, 2:2-4. In *Bahr al-Ra'iq* of Imam Ibn al-Nujaym, 2:216, it states:

(هي تمليك المال من فقير مسلم غيرها هاشمي ولا مولاه بشرط قطع المنفعة عن المملك كل لله تعالى) لقوله تعالى وآتوا الزكاة البقرة **43** والإيتاء هو التمليك ومراده تمليك جزء من ماله وهو ربع العشر أو ما يقوم مقامه

"[...] *Zakat* is obligatory because of the verse {**and pay the Zakat** [Q.2:43]} and 'paying the *zakat*' (*al-ita'*) is to give ownership and so means ownership of a part of one's wealth which is 2.5% or whatever in kind..."

- The definition as stated above has certain aspects to it:

1. <u>There must be real transference of ownership</u>: i.e. wealth passed from the hands of one person to the recipient. It cannot be a mere wish, unfulfilled promise or waiving of a debt and considering that to be the zakat, nor can the zakat money be spent on someone by the giver, etc. In short, zakat has to be *given*.

2. <u>Zakat must be offered to the poor and needy</u>: i.e. according to the Shari`a criterion not one's own judgment or assessment or government assessment criteria of 'poor' (see definition 3 below).

3. <u>Zakat must be offered to a Muslim and not non-Muslim</u>: because it is not a charity but a religiously mandatory transference of wealth.

4. <u>Zakat cannot be given to a descendent of Banu Hashim</u>: see below and fn.40.

5. <u>The person offering zakat cannot stand to gain from it materially</u>: i.e. there must be no reciprocal shared benefits accrued in giving the money. That is why zakat may not be given to one's parents, spouse or children.

- Imam al-Haskafi writes in *Durr al-Mukhtar Sharh Tanwir al-Absar*:

(وسبب لزوم أدائها توجه الخطاب) يعني قوله تعالى { آتوا الزَّكاة } (وشرطه) أي شرط
افتراض أدائها (حولان الحول) وهو في ملكه (وثمنية المال كالدراهم والدنانير) لتعينهما
للتجارة بأصل الخلقة فتلزم الزكاة كيفما أمسكهما ولو للنفقة

**"(What occasions the requirement to fulfil the payment
of zakat is the address of the Legislator)**, i.e. Allah's Most
high command in the verse {*and pay the zakat...*[Q. 2:277]}
(and its condition), meaning the condition of this obligation
to fulfil it **(is the passing of one year)** with the wealth in
one's possession **(that is a medium of exchange like
dirham and dinar)** because they are designated for trade in
their original creation. Therefore, *Zakat* is obligatory
regardless of why they the wealth was retained – even if it
was for financial support..."[11]

- Zakat then is an obligatory yearly liability on one's
  total wealth at a rate of 2.5% for the one who is
  sahib al-nisab (see 'nisab' section below).

- The amount accrued after a year does not give any
  consideration to how the amount was obtained, e.g.
  whether through:

1. A loan.
2. A gift.
3. Savings.
4. Inheritance.
5. Wage.
6. Payment.
7. Tax rebate,
8. Bonus, etc.

---

[11] al-Haskafi, *Durr al-Mukhtar*, 2:267 (= *Radd al-Muhtar*).

- The zakat payment is not on every item in one's possession but in 5 key areas and they are:

[1] Gold & silver:

1) Coins.
2) Jewellery.
3) Bullions.
4) Bars.
5) Utensils.
6) Ornaments.
7) Decorations.

[2] Money:

1) Cash.
2) Notes.
3) Coins.

[3] Merchandise:

1) Stocks.
2) Goods.
3) Saleable items.

[4] Agricultural produce

1) Slaughtered animals.
2) Harvested crops.

[5] Livestock:

1) Animals bred for commercial purposes.
2) Animals used for food, fibre (textiles) and labour

- In *Nur al-Idah* it has;

الأجناس التي تجب فيها الزكاة تجب الزكاة في الأجناس الآتية وهي السوائم الذهب
والفضة عروض التجارة الزروع والثمار المعدن والركاز

"The types [s: of wealth] upon which *zakat* is mandatory are
the following types: [1] livestock, [2] gold and silver; [3]
merchandise for trade; [4] agriculture and produce and [5]
treasure [s: e.g. war booty, etc.]..."[12]

[**Note: the basic rulings pertaining to agricultural produce
and livestock will form a separate appendix to this booklet
due to its immediate inapplicability to zakat rulings for the
average person].

[2] *Nisab* ('zakat threshold'): this is the amount of wealth
that qualifies a person to pay zakat, i.e. the quantified
minimum threshold. Anyone who qualifies for this threshold
is called *sahib al-nisab*. The % rate of the zakat is 2.5% of
total and aggregate zakatable assets. The *nisab* is held to be:

---

[12] al-Shurunbulali in *Nur al-Idah*, pp.346-347.

Type	Weight/Gram (g)	Appr. Currency Equivalent (£) (Fluctuates)
Gold (*dhahab*)	87.5 (= 20 *mithqal*)[13]	2800
Silver (*fidda*)	612.5 (200 *dirham*)[14]	600
Any Currency (£, $, €)	Equivalent to either the Gold or Silver weight above	*X*

General *Nisab* rulings:

1. For every 87.5g/20 *mithqal* of Gold, Fulan pays 17.4g/0.5 *mithqal* (i.e. ½). For every 612.5g/200 dirhams, Fulan pays 140g/5 dirhams.

2. If Fulan attains the *nisab* threshold and exceeds it by an additional fifth of the *nisab* value (i.e. 1/5), then he will pay proportionate to that amount due. Thus, for every 40 dirhams (= 1/5 of 200), Fulan pays 1 dirham.

---

[13] al-Marghinani, *al-Hidaya*, 1:174:

ليس فيما دون عشرين مثقالا من الذهب صدقة

"There is no *sadaqa* [s: i.e. *zakat* on wealth and assets] unless it amounts to 20 *mithqal* of gold [s: = 2.9 troy ounces]..."

[14] al-Marghinani, *al-Hidaya*, 1:174:

ليس فيما دون مائتي درهم صدقة

"There is no *sadaqa* [s: i.e. *zakat* on assets] unless it amounts to 200 dirhams [s: = 16.5 troy ounces of silver]..."

3. In reality, the *weight* of gold is taken into consideration (which is fixed), not the *value* of gold (which fluctuates).

4. The wealth amounting to the *nisab* threshold must be in the owner's possession for an entire year.

5. If in 2009 Fulan has wealth amounting to the *nisab* threshold and at 2010 also has the same amount or more, then zakat is due.

6. If in 2009 Fulan has wealth amounting to the *nisab* threshold but a few months later loses his wealth but then regains it before the year completes, zakat is still due because regardless of what happens in between the year, as long as one retains wealth amounting to the *nisab* threshold at the close of the year, zakat is due.

7. If a person has wealth amounting to the *nisab*, but has debts equal to or more than the *nisab*, no zakat is due.

8. If a person has wealth amounting to the *nisab*, but has debts less than the *nisab* such that having cleared all debts he still possess the *nisab* amount, zakat is due.

9. If one has gold or silver that amounts to the *nisab* threshold but it is mixed with other metals, zakat is still due.

10. If one has a little bit of gold or a little bit of silver and together it amounts to the *nisab* of either gold or silver, zakat is due.[15]

11. If one has the complete *nisab* of gold and the complete *nisab* of silver, it is better to offer the zakat on each separately. If one chooses to combine both, then whatever benefits the poor the most (*anfaʿ*) will be taken into consideration.

12. Cash is calculated according to the *nisab* of silver (612.5g/200 dirham); meaning if a person has enough cash that can purchase him 612.5g of silver, then zakat will be due.[16]

13. *Nisab hirman al-zakat*, i.e. possession of an amount of wealth in assets that precludes a person from

---

[15] al-Marghinani, *al-Hidaya*, 1:174:

وإذا كان الغالب على الورق الفضة فهو في حكم الفضة وإذا كان الغالب عليها الغش فهو في حكم العروض...

"If the money is mostly silver, then it will take the ruling of silver and if it is a mixture, then it takes the ruling of the material itself..."

[16] See *al-Fatawa al-Hindiyya*, 1:179:

وأما الفلوس فلا زكاة فيها إذا لم تكن للتجارة وإن كانت للتجارة فإن بلغت مائتين وجبت الزكاة كذا في المحيط...

"As for money (*fulus*), there is no *zakat* on it unless it is for trade. If it is for trade and it is the amount of 200 dirhams [s: which is the *nisab* of silver], *zakat* will be due as mentioned in *al-Muhit* [*al-Burhani*]..."

receiving zakat but does not obligate zakat on them either.[17]

[3] *Faqir/miskin* ('poor person'): one who is without essentials,[18] extremely poor,[19] begs for sustenance,[20] impoverished, with no money and does not fulfil the *nisab* category.[21] Even if one is healthy and earning.[22]

(هُوَ فَقِيرٌ، وَهُوَ مَنْ لَهُ أَدْنَى شَيْءٍ) أَيْ دُونَ نِصَابٍ أَوْ قَدْرُ نِصَابٍ غَيْرِ نَامٍ مُسْتَغْرِقٍ فِي الْحَاجَةِ.

"(He is considered poor, i.e. the one who has little possessions), i.e. who does not reach the *nisab* or a *nisab* amount; and he is without belongings or benefits and is in complete need."[23]

---

[17] For a discussion on this, see translator's note on al-Shurunbulali's *Maraqi al-Saʿadat*, p.139, fn.533.

[18] al-Kasani, *al-Badaʾiʿ al-Sanaʾiʿ*, 2:150.

[19] al-Kasani, *al-Badaʾiʿ al-Sanaʾiʿ*, 2:150.

[20] al-Kasani, *al-Badaʾiʿ al-Sanaʾiʿ*, 2:150.

[21] al-Shurunbulali in *Nur al-Idah*, p.356 differentiates between two recipients of zakat who are 'poor' and they are: [1] the *faqir* and [2] the *miskin*:

اما الفقير فهو : كل إنسان له مال لكنه لا يبلغ نصابا و أما المسكين فهو : كل إنسان لا يملك شيئا فهو أسوأ حال من الفقير...

"A needy person (*faqir*) is one who possesses some wealth but it does not amount to the *nisab* threshold whereas the destitute (*miskin*) is someone who possesses nothing at all and so the circumstance of the destitute is worse and more severe than the needy person..."

[22] However, it is better not to take *zakat* if one is healthy and able to earn a living; al-Kasani, *al-Badaʾiʿ al-Sanaʾiʿ*, 2:159.

[23] al-Haskafi, *Durr al-Mukhtar*, 2:339.

- Ibn `Abidin explains this clause in *Radd al-Muhtar*:

قوله: (مستغرق في الحاجة) كدار السكني وعبيد الخدمة وثياب البذلة وآلات الحرفة وكتب العلم للمحتاج إليها تدريسا أو حفظا أو تصحيحا كما مر أول الزكاة.

"(**To be in complete need**) like not having a place to say, a small servant to help, no basic clothes, no tools for trade, no books of knowledge needed for study or memorising or correction [s: and thus no real or material means of bettering one's situation]..."[24]

- Therefore, the items listed below are considered 'basic necessities' according to the Shari`a and so if anyone possesses them – regardless of their value – h/she will be not be considered 'rich' (*ghani*):

1. A place to stay.
2. Clothes.
3. Slaves/servants.
4. Furniture of a place.
5. Books for study.
6. Tools for a trade.
7. Any other essentials.

---

[24] Ibn `Abidin, *Radd al-Muhtar*, 2:339.

CHAPTER TWO

§4. Conditions pertaining to *Zakat*

- Imam al-Shurunbulali mentions the conditions (*shurut*) that obligates zakat in his primer entitled *Nur al-Idah*:

شروط وجوبها الإسلام والبلوغ والعقل والحرية وملك نصاب حولي فارغ عن الدين وحاجته
الأصلية نام ولو تقديرا...

"And the conditions for it being obligatory are: [1] attaining puberty; [2] discernment [s: i.e. rationality and sanity]; [3] being free [s: and not a slave]; [4] attaining the *nisab* threshold free from debt as well as basic and real necessities [s: and liabilities]..."[25]

- The conditions for <u>discharging</u> and fulfilling the zakat are:

- **One lunar Year**: the passing of one lunar year. In *Nur al-Idah*, it states:

شروط وجوب ادائها حولان الحول القمري على النصاب الأصلي بحيث يوجد في طرفي
الحول ولونقص في وسطه

"The condition for fulfilling the *zakat* is the passage of one lunar year (*hawl*) where one possesses the original/actual *nisab* amount and having it at the end of the year even if one did not possess it in the middle of the year..."[26]

---

[25] al-Shurunbulali, *Nur al-Idah*, p.120.
[26] al-Shurunbulali, *Nur al-Idah*, p.120.

- **Intention** (*niyya*) is a condition: In *Nur al-Idah*, it states:

ويشترط لصحة أداء الزكاة أحد ثلاثة أمور نية مقارنة للأداء أو نية مصاحبة لعزل المقدار الواجب أو التصدق بجميع ماله ولو من غيره نية الزكاة ولا يشترط أن يعلم الفقير أنها زكاة على الأصح حتى لو أعطاه شيئا وسماه هبة أو قرضا ونوى به الزكاة صحت

"The conditions that validates the fulfilment of *zakat* are three matters: making the intention at the time of paying the *zakat*; at the time of separating the required amount from the rest of his wealth or to entrust its payment to another [s: for it to be discharged] having made the intention of *zakat*. It is not a condition that the recipient of *zakat* knows that it is *zakat* being given to him according to the most correct position. It would even be permitted and valid to call the *zakat* being offered a 'gift' or a 'loan' while intending it as *zakat*..."[27]

- Because zakat is an act of worship (`*ibada*), it requires intention otherwise it will not be fulfilled.[28]

- The one paying the zakat must intend it as so and h/she has the time from up until the zakat is in the recipient's possession (as long as it has not been spent by the recipient).[29]

- Intention can be made at:

---

[27] al-Shurunbulali, *Nur al-Idah*, p.346.
[28] al-Zayla`i, *Tabyin al-Haqa'iq*, 1:257.
[29] al-Zayla`i, *Tabyin al-Haqa'iq*, 1:257.

[1] The time one pays the zakat to the recipient;

[2] The time when one devolves the responsibility of paying the zakat to one's legally appointed agent;

[3] The time one sets it aside for the future.[30]

---

[30] al-Zayla`i, *Tabyin al-Haqa'iq*, 1:257.

CHAPTER THREE

§5. Key *Zakat* Recipients

- The following categories of individuals are eligible recipients for zakat if they fulfil the conditions for it:

1. Foster-Parents.
2. Foster-children.
3. Father-in-law.
4. Mother-in-law.
5. Brothers.
6. Sisters.
7. Aunties.
8. Uncles.
9. Cousins.
10. Nephews.
11. Nieces.
12. Neighbours.
13. Clients (*mawali*).
14. Zakat collector (only if appointed by the Islamic State).[31]
15. A wayfarer/traveller who has no possessions for his journey.[32]
16. A person in debt.[33]
17. A soldier cut off from his troop or contingent.[34]
18. A pilgrim cut off from his group.[35]

---

[31] Which excludes any independent appointment, e.g. as an organisation. Cf. Ibn `Abidin, *Radd al-Muhtar*, 1:147.

[32] But if h/she has access to h/her wealth at home, then h/she may not be eligible for *zakat*. See al-Zayla`i, *Tabyin al-Haqa'iq*, 1:298.

[33] Such that h/her debt takes the wealth below the *nisab* threshold. al-Zayla`i, *Tabyin al-Haqa'iq*, 1:298.

[34] al-Shurunbulali, *Maraqi al-Sa`adat*, p.141.

[35] al-Shurunbulali, *Maraqi al-Sa`adat*, p.141.

19. {*Those whose hearts are to be reconciled...* [Q. 9:60]}.[36]

- In *Radd al-Muhtar* it states:

وَقُيِّدَ بِالْوِلَادِ لِجَوَازِهِ لِبَقِيَّةِ الْأَقَارِبِ كَالْإِخْوَةِ وَالْأَعْمَامِ وَالْأَخْوَالِ الْفُقَرَاءِ بَلْ هُمْ أَوْلَى؛ لِأَنَّهُ صِلَةٌ وَصَدَقَةٌ . وَفِي الظَّهِيرِيَّةِ : وَيَبْدَأُ فِي الصَّدَقَاتِ بِالْأَقَارِبِ، ثُمَّ الْمَوَالِي ثُمَّ الْجِيرَانِ، وَلَوْ دَفَعَ زَكَاتَهُ إِلَى مَنْ نَفَقَتُهُ وَاجِبَةٌ عَلَيْهِ مِنْ الْأَقَارِبِ جَازَ إِذَا لَمْ يَحْسِبْهَا مِنْ النَّفَقَةِ بَحْرٌ وَقَدَّمْنَاهُ مُوَضَّحًا أَوَّلَ الزَّكَاةِ . وَيَجُوزُ دَفْعُهَا لِزَوْجَةِ أَبِيهِ وَابْنِهِ وَزَوْجِ ابْنَتِهِ تَتَارْخَانِيَّةٌ

"[...] and it is mentioned in *al-Zahiriyya*: charity should begin with the close relatives, then the clients and then the neighbours. It is even permitted to offer *zakat* to any relative whose maintenance is mandatory for him if he has not yet counted it as maintenance as mentioned in *al-Bahr*... It is also permitted to offer *zakat* to his father's wife and son's wife and daughter's husband as in *al-Tatarkhaniyya*..."[37]

- The preferred serial for recipients of zakat are:

1. One's close relatives.
2. One's neighbours.
3. Residents of the local district/area.
4. Members of one's own profession.
5. General fellow citizens.[38]

---

[36] Since the time of Abu Bakr, this category for *zakat* is no longer applicable, see al-Zayla`i, *Tabyin al-Haqa'iq*, 1:299.
[37] Ibn `Abidin, *Radd al-Muhtar*, 2:346-347.
[38] al-Shurunbulali, *Maraqi al-Sa`adat*, p.143.

§6. Key Non-*Zakat* Recipients

- The following categories are **not** eligible recipients of *zakat*:

1. Non-Muslims and non-Muslim citizens of the Islamic state as well as those at war with Muslims (*harbi*).[39]
2. A deceased person and any burial procedures for h/her.
3. Any slave or a slave who is bought in order to be emancipated.
4. Any rich/wealthy person whether adult or child which includes their slaves.
5. One's own self.
6. One's spouse.
7. One's father and grandfather, mother and grandmother.
8. One's children and grandchildren.
9. A member of Banu Hashim (the family and clan of the Messenger of Allah) which includes Sayyids of today.[40]

---

[39] Ibn `Ali al-Haddadi, *al-Jawharat al-Nayyira*, 3:286:

وَاعْلَمْ أَنَّهُ لَا يَجُوزُ دَفْعُهَا إِلَى ثَمَانِيَةِ الْغَنِيِّ وَوَلَدِ الْغَنِيِّ الصَّغِيرِ وَزَوْجَةِ الْغَنِيِّ إِذَا كَانَ لَهَا مَهْرٌ عَلَيْهِ وَعَبْدِ الْغَنِيِّ الْقَنِّ وَدَفْعُهَا إِلَى وَلَدِهِ وَوَلَدِ وَلَدِهِ وَأَبَوَيْهِ وَأَجْدَادِهِ وَأَحَدِ الزَّوْجَيْنِ إِلَى الْآخَرِ وَبَنِي هَاشِمٍ وَبَنِي هَاشِمٍ وَالْكَافِرِ سَوَاءٌ كَانَ ذِمِّيًّا أَوْ حَرْبِيًّا

"[...] and no *zakat* is given to a non-Muslim even if he is a citizen of the Islamic State or at war with it..."

[40] In al-Zayla`is *Tabyin al-Haqa'iq*, 1:303 it has:

لَا يَجُوزُ دَفْعُهَا إِلَى بَنِي هَاشِمٍ لِقَوْلِهِ – عَلَيْهِ الصَّلَاةُ وَالسَّلَامُ – «إِنَّ هَذِهِ الصَّدَقَاتِ إِنَّمَا أَوْسَاخُ النَّاسِ وَإِنَّهَا لَا تَحِلُّ لِمُحَمَّدٍ وَلَا لِآلِ مُحَمَّدٍ» رَوَاهُ مُسْلِمٌ وَقَالَ – عَلَيْهِ الصَّلَاةُ وَالسَّلَامُ – «نَحْنُ أَهْلُ بَيْتٍ لَا تَحِلُّ لَنَا الصَّدَقَةُ» رَوَاهُ الْبُخَارِيُّ

- In al-Quduri's *Mukhtasar* with its legal commentary by al-Ghunaymi, it states:

ولا يجوز أن يدفع الزكاة إلى ذمي، ولا يبني بها مسجدٌ، ولا يكفن بها ميتٌ، ولا يشتري بها رقبةٌ تتعتق، ولا تدفع إلى غني، ولا يدفع المزكي زكاته إلى أبيه وجده وإن علا ولا إلى ولده وولد ولده وإن سفل ولا إلى امرأته، ولا تدفع المرأة إلى زوجها ولا يدفع إلى مكاتبه ولا مملوكه ولا مملوك غنيٍ ولا ولد غني إذا كان صغيراً، ولا تدفع إلى بني هاشمٍ، وهم. آل عليٍ وآل عباسٍ وآل جعفرٍ وآل عقيلٍ وآل حارث بن عبد المطلب ومواليهم،

"It is not permitted to pay *zakat* to a *dhimmi*, nor is it permitted to establish a Mosque with it, nor is it permitted to bury and shroud a deceased with it, nor may one purchase a slave with it in order to emancipate and free it; one may not pay a rich person with it; a person who must pay *zakat* may not offer it to his father and grandfather even if both are old in age nor to his child and grandchild even if both are very young; nor may he offer it to his wife; a wife may not offer [s: the *zakat* money] to her husband, or a *mukatab* slave, or an owned slave, a rich person's slave or a rich child when it is small; nor may it be offered to a member of Banu Hashim, the family of `Ali [Allah be pleased with him], the family of Ibn `Abbas, the family of Ja`far, the family of `Aqil, the family of Harith b. `Abd al-Muttalib and their clients (*mawalihim*)[41]..."[42]

"It is not permitted to offer *zakat* to the members of Banu Hashim because he (upon him be peace) said: '**These *sadaqat* are for the less fortunate persons and it not permitted for Muhammad or the family of Muhammad**'. Narrated by Muslim. And he – upon him be peace – also said: '**We are a household and there is no *sadaqa* for us**'. Narrated by al-Bukhari..." For a legal discussion, see Alahazrat's *al-Zahr al-Basim fi Hurmat al-Zakat `ala Bani Hashim*, pp.272-290.

[41] What is meant by "*mawalihim*" ('their clients') is:

CHAPTER FOUR

§7. Non-*Zakatable* Areas

- Zakat may not be given on non-persons, devotional actions (*`ibadat*), physical structures and realities and where there is no ownership involved such as:

1. Infrastructure, e.g. bridges, roads, highways, motorways, irrigation routes, water pipes, etc.

2. Public/natural resources, e.g. Canals, rivers, lakes, ponds, seas, reservoirs, etc.

3. Buildings, e.g. houses, flats, complexes, hospitals, Mosques, universities, schools, Islamic *madrasa*, etc.

4. Acts of worship, e.g. Hajj, Jihad, Prayer, etc.

- In *al-Fatawa al-Hindiyya* it states:

وَلَا يَجُوزُ أَنْ يَبْنِيَ بِالزَّكَاةِ الْمَسْجِدَ وَكَذَا الْقَنَاطِرُ وَالسِّقَايَاتُ وَإِصْلَاحُ الطَّرَقَاتِ وَكَرْيُ الْأَنْهَارِ وَالْحَجُّ وَالْجِهَادُ وَكُلُّ ما لَا تَمْلِيكَ فيه

"It is not permitted to erect a Mosque with *zakat* money. Neither can it be used to build bridges, canals, irrigation and

---

(وَمَوَالِيهِمْ) أَيْ مُعْتَقِي بَنِي هَاشِمٍ لِمَا تَقَرَّرَ أَنَّ مَوْلَى الْقَوْمِ مِنْهُمْ

"...(**and their clients**) means those who were freed from Banu Hashim because it is affirmed and upheld that a person who is a client of a people is from them..." See Mulla Khusru, *al-Durar al-Hukkam Sharh Ghurar al-Ahkam*, 1:91. Although Imam al-Tahawi considered it permitted to offer them *zakat* (cf. al-Shurunbulali, *Maraqi al-Sa`adat*, p.142).
[42] al-Quduri, *al-Mukhtasar*, pp.165-166 (= al-Ghunaymi's *al-Lubab*).

watering holes, road repairs, rivers, Hajj, Jihad or anything in which there is no ownership (*al-tamlik*) involved...”[43]

- There is also no zakat on items that are owned but are required of necessity or daily need such as:

  1. Cars.
  2. Bikes.
  3. Motorcycles.
  4. Books.
  5. Clothes.
  6. Dwellings (e.g. one's room, house, etc.).
  7. Servants.

- Ibn ‘Abidin writes:

وقد أجمع الفقهاء على أنه ليس في دور السكنى، وثياب البدن، وأثاث المنازل، ودواب الركوب، وعبيد الخدمة، وسلاح الاستعمال زكاة لأنها مشغولة بالحاجة الأصلية، وليست بنامية

“There is no *zakat* on: a room or dwelling, the clothes on one's body, the furnishings of a home, riding beasts and animals neither on servants nor on weapons that are used. This is because [s: all of these means] are for essential purposes and not for betterment, advancement or increase...”[44]

- There is generally no zakat on personal possessions and belongings such as:

---

[43] See *al-Fatawa al-Hindiyya*, 1:188.
[44] Ibn ‘Abidin, *Radd al-Muhtar*, 2:262.

1. Rings (unless gold and silver).
2. Non-gold and silver jewellery (e.g. diamonds, platinum, metals, etc.).
3. Watches (unless and silver).
4. Mobile phones.
5. Accessories (e.g. hats, scarfs, etc. unless woven with gold and silver).
6. Electronic devices.
7. Pots, pans, etc.
8. Utensils (unless made of Gold and silver).
9. Pets.
10. Etc.

- There is also no zakat on the actual items that are rented/hired out or loaned out/borrowed such as:

1. Houses.
2. Flats.
3. Cars/vehicles.
4. Spaces.
5. Items. Etc.

Note: The key rule to remember however on items is that if an item was purchased with the *intention of resale or for trade*, then the item will be subject to zakat.

CHAPTER FIVE

§8. Zakat and the State[45]

- One of the permanent revenue streams for the Khilafah treasury (*bayt al-mal*) is zakat.[46]

- Zakat is one of the means through which wealth is circulated within the different tiers of the economy as well as for achieving a balance of monetary distribution.[47]

- The state will ensure that the eligible recipients of zakat (outlined above in §5) actually receive it. This is one of the functions of the Khalifah.[48]

- The Khilafah must deposit zakat revenues in state treasury holdings in order to distribute it to those eligible and must not spend it on economic matters of the state, e.g. to settle debts and fund infrastructure projects.[49]

---

[45] For detailed account of the state funds and zakat, see Sh. `Abd al-Qadim Zallum's *al-Amwal fi Dawlat al-Khilafah*, pp.121-162 (English).

[46] al-Nabhani, *Nizam al-Iqtisadi*, pp.239-240 (Arabic) and pp.220-224 (English).

[47] al-Nabhani, *Nizam al-Iqtisadi*, p.58 (Arabic) and p.64 (English).

[48] al-Nabhani, *Nizam al-Iqtisadi*, pp.240-242 (Arabic) and pp.225-227 (English).

[49] al-Nabhani, *Nizam al-Iqtisadi*, pp. (Arabic) and pp.227-228 (English).

CHAPTER SIX

§9. Rulings for Zakat and Businesses

General Rules:

1. *Zakat* on business have the following conditions:

- It must be lawful assets.
- A year must elapse (*hawlan al-hawl*).
- The *nisab* quantum must be reached.
- One must have ownership over the assets (*milk al-tamm*).
- One's assets must be productive (e.g. potential to increase - *al-nama'*).
- Business intention (*`urud al-tijara*).

2. In terms of partnership, *zakat* is given according to the partner's % owned in the partnership. For example, if A owns 50% share in a partnership or company through investment, then A must pay *zakat* on 50% of the company/partnership's merchandise/stock/trade goods.[50] Thus, if the total value of the merchandise is £5000, then A will pay *zakat* on £2,500 if that fulfils the *zakat* quantum.[51]

---

[50] This is any item bought for the intention to be *traded*, i.e. bought and sold.

[51] al-Sarakhsi, *al-Mabsut*, 2:185:

وَالشَّرِيكُ الْمُفَاوِضُ وَالْعَنَّانُ وَغَيْرُ ذَلِكَ كُلُّهُمْ سَوَاءٌ فِي حُكْمِ الصَّدَقَةِ؛ لِأَنَّ وُجُوبَهَا بِاعْتِبَارِ حَقِيقَةِ الْمِلْكِ وَغِنَى الْمَالِكِ بِهِ وَلَا مِلْكَ لِلشَّرِيكِ فِي نَصِيبِ شَرِيكِهِ مُفَاوِضًا كَانَ أَوْ غَيْرُهُ

al-Fatawa al-Hindiyya, 2:336:

3. Only merchandise is subject to *zakat*, not:

- Furniture.
- Fixtures.
- Fittings.
- Hardware.
- Machinery.
- Computers.
- Any business asset that is **not** for sale.

4. The value of the merchandise, stock or saleable assets must be according to the market value and not arbitrary designations (e.g. one's own estimation or guesswork).

5. As a principle, if one has stocks/merchandise as well as cash, he should combine the value of both. If the total value reaches the *nisab* (zakat quantum), he will give 2.5% of that total and combined value.

- Imam al-Kasani in *al-Bada'i` al-Sana'i`* states:

قَالَ أَصْحَابُنَا: إِنَّهُ يُعْتَبَرُ فِي حَالِ الشَّرِكَةِ مَا يُعْتَبَرُ فِي حَالِ الِانْفِرَادِ وَهُوَ كَمَالُ النِّصَابِ فِي حَقِّ كُلِّ وَاحِدٍ مِنْهُمَا فَإِنْ كَانَ نَصِيبُ كُلِّ وَاحِدٍ مِنْهُمَا يَبْلُغُ نِصَابًا تَجِبُ الزَّكَاةُ وَإِلَّا فَلَا

فَإِنْ أَذِنَ كُلُّ وَاحِدٍ مِنْهُمَا لِصَاحِبِهِ أَنْ يُؤَدِّيَ الزَّكَاةَ عَنْهُ فَأَدَّيَا مَعًا ضَمَّنَ كُلُّ وَاحِدٍ مِنْهُمَا نَصِيبَ صَاحِبِهِ عَلِمَ أَوْ لَمْ يَعْلَمْ عِنْدَ أَبِي حَنِيفَةَ – رَحِمَهُ اللَّهُ تَعَالَى –، كَذَا فِي الْكَافِي –، وَلَوْ أَدَّيَا أَدَاءً مُتَعَاقِبًا ضَمِنَ الثَّانِي، عَلِمَ بِأَدَاءِ صَاحِبِهِ أَمْ لَا، عِنْدَ الْإِمَامِ – رَضِيَ اللَّهُ تَعَالَى عَنْهُ –، كَذَا فِي النَّهْرِ الْفَائِقِ.

"Our companions say: what is considered in the case of a partnership (*al-sharika*) is the same as that considered in case of an individual which is reaching of the *nisab* quantum with regards to each one of them. If the share of each partner reaches the *nisab* quantum, *zakat* is mandatory on him otherwise it is not..."[52]

---

[52] See al-Kasani, *al-Bada'i` al-Sana'i`*, 2:29.

CHAPTER SEVEN

§10. Zakat and Land

- There is no *zakat* on commercial land for the one who owns it.

- This also means there is no *zakat* on commercial complexes built on that land (e.g. Properties, buildings, structures, etc).

- However, any *income* from the land, such as through agricultural produce or from rentals from the land (e.g. via hotels, apartments, resorts, etc. that are built on it) have to be added to the yearly savings that will then be zakatable if kept for over a year.

- There is *zakat* on the proceeds from selling a land from when the money is received.

- There is *zakat* on the land if it is bought to be immediately sold because it will be considered as stock-in-trade.[53]

---

[53] In al-Haddadi al-Yamani's *Jawharat al-Nayyira*, 1:478 it states:

(الزكاة واجبة في عروض التجارة كائنة ما كانت) أي سواء كانت من جنس ما تجب فيه الزكاة كالسوائم أو من غيره كالثياب والحمير

"(*Zakat* is mandatory on trading good wherever it is located) meaning regardless of whether it is an item that is obligatorily zakatable or not like flocks and herds or other than that like clothes and donkeys..."

CHAPTER EIGHT

§11. Zakat and Debts

Below are two classical Hanafi texts on *Zakat* and debt categories. Understanding them is relevant to the ruling on *Zakat* with regards to loans (*qard*), debts (*dayn*) owed or any other liability.

Text 1:[54]

وجملة الكلام في الديون أنها على ثلاث مراتب في قول أبي حنيفة : دين قوي، ودين ضعيف، ودين وسط كذا قال عامة مشايخنا أما القوي فهو الذي وجب بدلا عن مال التجارة كثمن عرض التجارة من ثياب التجارة، وعبيد التجارة، أو غلة مال التجارة ولا خلاف في وجوب الزكاة فيه إلا أنه لا يخاطب بأداء شيء من زكاة ما مضى ما لم يقبض أربعين درهما، فكلما قبض أربعين درهما أدى درهما واحدا وعند أبي يوسف ومحمد كلما قبض شيئا يؤدي زكاته قل المقبوض أو كثر . وأما الدين الضعيف فهو الذي وجب له بدلا عن شيء سواء وجب له بغير صنعه كالميراث، أو بصنعه كما لوصية، أو وجب بدلا عما ليس بمال كالمهر، وبدل الخلع، والصلح عن القصاص، وبدل الكتابة ولا زكاة فيه ما لم يقبض كله ويحول عليه الحول بعد القبض . وأما الدين الوسط فما وجب له بدلا عن مال ليس للتجارة كثمن عبد الخدمة، وثمن ثياب البذلة والمهنة وفيه روايتان عنه، ذكر في الأصل أنه تجب فيه الزكاة قبل القبض لكن لا يخاطب بالأداء ما لم يقبض مائتي درهم فإذا قبض مائتي درهم زكى لما مضى، وروى ابن سماعة عن أبي يوسف عن أبي حنيفة أنه لا زكاة فيه حتى يقبض المائتين ويحول عليه الحول من وقت القبض وهو أصح الروايتين عنه

---

[54] See al-Kasani, *al-Bada'i` al-Sana'i`*, 2:292.

Text 2:[55]

(و) اعلم أن الديون عند الإمام ثلاثة قوي ومتوسط وضعيف (فتجب) زكاتها إذا تم نصابا
وحال الحول لكن لا فورا بل (عند قبض أربعين درهما من الدين) القوي كقرض (وبدل
مال تجارة) فكلما قبض أربعين درهما يلزمه درهم (و) عند قبض (مائتين منه لغيرها)
أي من بدل مال لغير تجارة وهو المتوسط كثمن سائمة وعبيد خدمة ونحوهما مما هو
مشغول بحوائجه الأصلية كطعام وشراب وأملاك ويعتبر ما مضى من الحول قبل القبض في
الأصح ومثله ما لو ورث دينا على رجل (و) عند قبض (مائتين مع حولان الحول بعده)
أي بعد القبض (من) دين ضعيف وهو (بدل غير مال) كمهر ودية وبدل كتابة وخلع

Debts:

- There are generally three types of debts the scholars have discussed:

[1] *Immediate* debt, i.e. that which is owed right away or urgently.

[2] *Deferred* debt, i.e. that debt which is owed later or in some later specified time.

[3] *Long-term* debts, i.e. debts over a number of years.

- The Hanafi scholars have different opinions on the issue. Some say all debts prevent a person from paying *zakat*. Others say only immediate debts prevent the payment of *zakat* and not the deferred debt. What seems to be the more correct opinion of

---

[55] al-Haskafi, *Durr al-Mukhtar*, 3:236.

the school is that deferred and long term debts are not factored in when calculating *zakat*. In other words, they are not zakatable.

- Debt is essentially viewed by Hanafi jurists as money not owned by a person but owed to others and so if one does not actually own h/her wealth, it cannot be zakatable.

- If a person possesses the full *nisab* and also has personal debts which equal the *nisab*, then in such a case *zakat* will not be mandatory to pay.

- If debts are such that if as person were to fulfil his debts he will have a remainder of wealth which will equal the *nisab*, then *zakat* will be mandatory on him.

In terms of *zakat* and long-term debts such as mortgages or large loans, one does not deduct from the total *zakat* amount the entire sum of the mortgage or loan, nor does one deduct the entire sum of one year's payments but only the figure of the monthly payment that is due.

CHAPTER NINE

§12. Rulings for *Sadaqat al-Fitr*

- Imam al-Shurunbulali outlines the basic rulings regarding the *sadaqat al-fitr*:

SADAQAT AL-FITR: Its definition is: the payment of charity by a Muslim on the Day of `Id al-Fitr to those eligible for the *zakat*.

The wisdom behind it: The great wisdom behind this injunction has been given by our beloved Prophet (Allah bless him and grant him peace) during the 2nd year of the Hijra such which includes: to offer money to the poor so they do not have to beg on the great day of `Id so as to include them in rejoicing and being happy with the rest of the Muslims. It is to also purify the wealth of the one who had been fasting [s: during the month of Ramadan) after having purified his body through the fast as well as to redress any deficiencies in his fast. The Messenger of Allah

صدقة الفطر تعريفها هي صدقة يعطيها المسلم في يوم عيد الفطر لمن تصرف إليهم الزكاة

حكمتها أمرنا بها سيدنا النبي صلى الله عليه وسلم في السنة الثانية من الهجرة لحكم جليلة وأغراض نبيله منها إغناء الفقراء عن ذل السؤال في هذا اليوم العظيم إدخال الفرح والسرور عليهم في هذا اليوم الذي يفرح فيه المسلمون جميعا تطهير مال الصائم بعد أن تطهر جسده بالصوم جبر ما عساه أن يكون من خلل في صومه قال سيدنا رسول الله صلى الله عليه وسلم زكاة الفطر طهرة للصائم من اللغو والرفث

ركنها تمليكها لمن تعطى اليه فلا تكفي الإباحة فيها سببها رأس يمونه ويلي عليه

(Allah bless him and grant him peace) said: '**the** *zakat al-fitr* **is a purification from vain and pointless matters as well as filthy speech for the one who fasts'**.[56]

Its pillar (*rukn*) is to ensure full ownership for the recipient [s: of the *sadaqa*]; merely giving permission is not sufficient [...] he pays it himself from his own money, for his small children, the poor children, his servant, as well as his *mudabbar* and *umm walad* slaves.

The conditions that make it mandatory [s:for a person to receive *sadaqat al-fitr*] are: [1] being Muslim; [2] being free and [3] possessing in excess of the *nisab* amount hence over and above one's essential needs regardless of whether or not there was increase on that or whether or not a year had passed and he possessed the *nisab* amount.

The time that obligates it: this

أي شخصه وما كان في معناه ممن يمونه ويلي عليه ولاية كاملة فيخرجها عن نفسه وأولاده الصغار الفقراء وعبيده للخدمة ومدبره وأم ولده

شروط وجوبها الإسلام والحرية وملك نصاب فاضل عن حاجته الأصلية سواء أكان ناميا أم لا وسواء أحال عليه الحول أم لا

وقت وجوبها تجب بطلوع فجر يوم الفطر فمن مات قبله أو افتقر أو أسلم أو ولد أو اغتنى بعده لا تجب عليه ويصح أداؤها مقدما عن يوم الفطر أو مؤخرا عنه إلا أنه يستحب أداؤها قبل الخروج الى المصلى ولا تسقط بهلاك المال بعد الوجوب

الاصناف التي تخرج منها الأصناف التي تخرج منها أحد أربعة البر والشعير والتمر والزبيب

---

[56] See al-Tabrizi, *Mishkat al-Masabih*, 1:570.

is when the sun rises on the day of `Id al-Fitr. So, anyone who dies before that time or becomes impoverished, becomes Muslim, is born or becomes rich *after* that time, it is not mandatory on them to pay it. It is valid to pay it in advance of the `Id day [s: by up to a month according to some opinions] or after it although it is better to discharge it before leaving for the place of Prayer. Loss of wealth does not excuse one from paying it [s: after it becomes mandatory for those to discharge it and neither does delaying it excuse a person although a person would be committing an offence for doing so, i.e. it is *makruh tanzihi*].[57]

<u>The types from which *sadaqa* may be paid</u>: The types of things from which *sadaqa* may be paid can be one of four: [1] wheat, [2] barley, [3] dates and [4] raisins.

<u>The required amount</u>: And the

مقدار الواجب ومقدار الواجب نصف
صاع من البر أو دقيقه أو سويقه وصاع
كامل من الشعير أو التمر أو الزبيب
والصاع يعادل غرام تقريبا إخراج القيمة
ويجوز إخراج القيمة بل هي أفضل اذا
كانت أنفع للفقير

---

[57] Shaykh Zadah, *Majma` al-Anhur*, 1:228.

required amount is half a *sa`* of wheat [s: = 1.6kg) or flour or *sawiqa* (a mixture of wheat and barley); one complete *sa`* [s: = 3.2kg] of barley or dates or raisins. The *sa`* approximates to a *gharam*.

It is permissible to pay *sadaqat al-fitr* in cash that is equivalent to any of the above. In fact, it would be better if it was more beneficial to the poor...”[58]

Summary:

- From the above passage, therefore, we have the following summarised rulings:

Hikam (wisdoms):

○ The wisdoms (*hikam*) of *sadaqat al-fitr* are: 1) enriching the poor; 2) including them in the celebration of `Id and 3) purifying any deficiencies in the fast.[59]

---

[58] al-Shurunbullai, *Nur al-Idah*, 1:71-72.
[59] al-Kasani, *al-Bada'i` al-Sana'i`*, 2:543.

Payers:

- o It is obligatory for anyone who is: 1) Muslim, 2) free and 3) holds in excess of the *nisab* amount.[60]
- o A husband will be responsible to pay for: 1) any poor minor children, 2) any servants and 3) slaves.[61]
- o A husband is not required to pay for: 1) wife and 2) mature children because they are liable to discharge it themselves but it is permitted for him to do so with their permission.[62]

- o If a child possesses the *nisab*, then the father may dispense of the *sadaqa* on h/her behalf under the laws of guardianship.[63]

Recipients:

- o <u>The recipients</u> of the *sadaqat al-fitr* are:

1. The poor (*fuqara'*).
2. The destitute and helpless (*al-masakin*).
3. Those employed by the Khalifah to collect the zakat (*amilin `alayha*).
4. New Muslims whose hearts have been reconciled to Islam (*al-mu'allaf al-qulub*).
5. Those agreed to free a slave (*al-riqab*).
6. Those in debt (*al-gharimin*).
7. Those fighting in the way of Allah (*fi sabil Allah*).
8. Those cut off from their land (*ibn al-sabil*).

---

[60] Ibn al-Humam, *Sharh Fath al-Qadir*, 2:285-286.
[61] Ibn al-Humam, *Sharh Fath al-Qadir*, 2:285-286.
[62] Ibn al-Humam, *Sharh Fath al-Qadir*, 2:289-290.
[63] See *al-Fatawa al-Hindiyya*, 1:211.

Time of payment:

- *Sadaqat al-fitr* is generally offered at the closing of Ramadan.
- It becomes obligatory to dispense it at the break of dawn.[64]
- It is better to pay it after *Fajr* before the `Id Prayer.[65]
- It can be paid days after `Id.

What to give:

- It is better to pay the *sadaqa* in what benefits the poor the most (*anfa`*) in order to fulfil the goal (*maqsid*) of the *hukm*.[66]
- One may discharge the *sadaqat al-fitr* either by paying:

1) 1 *sa`* of barley or
2) 1 *sa`* of dates or
3) ½ *sa`* of wheat or
4) 1 *sa`* raisins.[67]

- The value of the above in cash may be given.[68]

---

[64] al-Kasani, *al-Bada'i` al-Sana'i*, 2:544.
[65] al-Kasani, *al-Bada'i` al-Sana'i*, 2:544.
[66] al-Kasani, *al-Bada'i` al-Sana'i*, 2:543.
[67] al-Kasani, *al-Bada'i` al-Sana'i*, 2:540. The values of each will be determined according to the area and locality. Ibn al-Nujaym, *al-Bahr al-Ra'iq*, 2:400.
[68] Ibn `Abidin, *Radd al-Muhtar*, 3:322.

CHAPTER TEN

§13. Rulings for Miscellaneous and Contemporary Issues

<u>Some Miscellaneous Rulings:</u>

- **Adding zakatable assets together to form the *nisab***: the Shari`a has designated each zakatable asset with a quantum, i.e. the *nisab* threshold so they should not be lumped together in order to reach the *nisab* quantum. Thus, livestock and trade stocks should not be added together until a *nisab* figure is reached. Each should be kept separate. **Example**: If A reached the *nisab* threshold by amassing assets to the value of 87.5g of gold, not by say adding different animals together to get 40 items, then regardless of whether any other assets are added, zakat is due. However, any source of cash or money can be grouped together to ascertain the *nisab* threshold on that total amount.

- **Excessive zakat**: it is disliked to give a person so much zakat such that h/she becomes qualified now to give zakat. However, the zakat will stand paid and complete.

- **Insufficient zakat:** it is disliked to offer too little zakat such that one falls in need again for that day.

- **Zakat in kind**: *zakat al-mal* ('zakat wealth') may be given in kind, meaning not just monetary value of gold and silver but stocks, goods and merchandise of the zakat value.

- **Zakat and vouchers**: It is permitted to give vouchers as a form of zakat. However, because vouchers are not wealth in itself but a form of assigned debt against the issuer of the voucher, zakat will not be considered discharged until the recipient receives the goods the voucher allows. **Example**: A gives a food voucher as a form of zakat to B (who is eligible for zakat). B will not be considered a proper beneficiary of the zakat – and A's zakat will not be considered discharged – until B actually receives the food in his possession. Mere receipt of the voucher therefore will not be considered a discharged zakat.

- **Previous unpaid zakat**: previous unpaid zakat is treated as a liability and hence has to be added to one's next or current zakat anniversary date.[69]

- **Zakat and *haram* income**: there is in general no zakat on unacceptable means of income according to the Shari`a like interest based income, income from deceit, stolen goods, bribery, forgery, etc.[70]

- **Husband and zakat**: A husband may discharge the zakat on behalf of his wife <u>with her permission</u>.[71]

---

[69] Ibn `Abidin, *Radd al-Muhtar*, 2:282.
[70] Mufti Aziz al-Rahman, `*Aziz al-Fatawa*, 2:24.
[71] Ibn `Abidin, *Radd al-Muhtar*, 2:269:

قال في البحر ولو تصدق عنه بأمره جاز ويرجع بما دفع عند أبي يوسف وعند محمد لا يرجع إلا بشرط الرجوع اه تأمل ثم قال في التاترخانية أو وجدت دلالة الإذن بالخلط كما جرت العادة بالإذن من أرباب الحنطة بخلط ثمن الغلات ... فيه إشارة إلى أنه لا يشترط الدفع من عين مال الزكاة ولذا لو أمر غيره بالدفع عنه جاز كما قدمناه

- **Wife and zakat**: In the Hanafi School, a wife cannot give her husband zakat. This is the position of Imam Abu Hanifa.[72]

- **Zakat representative**: It is permitted to appoint a person to distribute the zakat on one's behalf to the eligible recipients based on the rulings related to *wakala* (agency).[73]

- **Zakat and organisations**: It is permitted to appoint an organisation to distribute the zakat on one's behalf to the eligible recipients based on the rulings

---

"[...] in it is an indication that it is not a condition that *zakat* has to be paid by the person himself and so if he wanted to, he can order another to pay on his behalf as we explained earlier."

[72] al-Marghinani, *al-Hidaya*, 1:111:

ولا تدفع المرأة إلى زوجها

"And the wife does not give *zakat* to her husband..." See also *al-Fatawa al-Hindiyya* 1:189 and al-Mawsili, *al-Ikhtiyar*, 1:120 respectively:

ولا تدفع المرأة إلى زوجها عند أبي حنيفة رحمه الله تعالى كذا في الهداية...

(ولا إلى زوجته) لأن المنافع بينهم متصلة، ويعد غنيا بمال زوجته. قال تعالى: {ووجدك عائلا فأغنى} [الضحى: 8] " قالوا: بمال خديجة – رضي الله عنها – وكذلك الزوجة لا تدفع إلى زوجها لأنها تعد غنية باعتبار ما لها عليه من النفقة والكسوة، ولأنهما أصل الولاد، وما يتفرع من هذا الأصل يمنع صرف الزكاة فكذا الأصل، ولهذا يرث كل واحد منهما من الآخر من غير حجب كقرابة الولاد. وقال أبو يوسف ومحمد: تدفع إلى زوجها، «لقوله – عليه الصلاة والسلام – لزينب امرأة ابن مسعود وقد سألته عن التصدق على زوجها: " لك أجران: أجر الصدقة، وأجر الصلة». قلنا: هو محمول على صدقة التطوع لما بينا من اتصال المنافع بينهما وذلك جائز عنده.

[73] Ibn `Abidin, *Radd al-Muhtar*, 2:269.

pertaining to *wakala* (legal agency).[74] However, utmost care must be taken to ensure the representatives fulfil the zakat payment otherwise the zakat will not stand fulfilled.

- **Informing zakat recipients**: When giving zakat, one should avoid informing the recipients that it is zakat in case it injures the pride, or causes embarrassment. However, doing so is not prohibited.

- **Zakat sent abroad**: It is permissible to send zakat payment abroad to poorer countries. The obligation will be considered discharged.[75]

- **Zakat and dawah projects**: it is not permissible to give zakat for dawah projects or to dawah channels. Zakat is restricted to 8 recipients mentioned in Q. 9:60 and no-one else. It is not possible to interpret "in the way of Allah" {*fi sabil Allah...*} as dawah channels or dawah projects because it refers to those fighting in the way of Allah as well as the poor seeking to perform Hajj. Allah knows best.[76]

- **Delaying zakat**: One should not delay paying the zakat for its year unless with a valid reason (`udhr`) as one will be considered sinful in such a case requiring repentance (*tawba*). Usually, one has until the next zakat anniversary date to discharge the zakat.[77]

---

[74] Ibn `Abidin, *Radd al-Muhtar*, 2:269.

[75] Mufti Ludhianvi, *Ahsan al-Fatawa*, 4:259.

[76] al-Kasani, *al-Bada'i` al-Sana'i`*, 2:39f and Ibn `Abidin, *Radd al-Muhtar*, 2:339.

[77] Alahazrat, *Tajalli al-Mishkat li-Anar As'ilat al-Zakat*, pp.76-169.

- **Zakat and animals**: Zakat money may not be spent on animals and animal welfare because a human being has to be made owner of the money.

Some Contemporary financial issues:

- **Zakat on deposits**: If one has ownership over the rental deposit amount, then it must be added to the total zakatable amount. Otherwise it is not because the condition for zakat on wealth is to have ownership and control over the wealth.[78]

- **Zakat on rental income**: Zakat will be given on any rental income but not on the value of a property. **Example**: If A owns a flat or other properties, then any rental income from these properties will be added to the total zakat liability inventory of A.

---

[78] See *al-Fatawa al-Hindiyya*, 1:172:

وَمِنْهَا الْمِلْكُ التَّامُّ وهو ما اجْتَمَعَ فيه الْمِلْكُ وَالْيَدُ وَأَمَّا إذَا وُجِدَ الْمِلْكُ دُونَ الْيَدِ كَالصَّدَاقِ قبل الْقَبْضِ أو وُجِدَ الْيَدُ دُونَ الْمِلْكِ كَمِلْكِ الْمُكَاتَبِ وَالْمَدْيُونِ لَا تَجِبُ فيه الزَّكَاةُ كَذَا في السِّرَاجِ الْوَهَّاجِ وَأَمَّا الْمَبِيعُ قبل الْقَبْضِ فَقِيلَ لَا يَكُونُ نِصَابًا وَالصَّحِيحُ أَنَّهُ يَكُونُ نِصَابًا كَذَا في مُحِيطِ السَّرَخْسِيِّ

"And another condition is to have complete ownership [s: over one's wealth or assets] which is to have ownership and possession together. If ownership exists but no possession like in the case of a marital dower before possessing it or possession exists without ownership as in the case of a *mukatab*'s ownership [s: of something] or a debtor's ownership then no *zakat* is obligatory as mentioned in *al-Siraj al-Wahhaj*. As for the commodity that is not yet delivered, it is said that it is not part of the *nisab* but the most correct view is that it is..."

- **Zakat on stock investments**: zakat will be levied on stock investments because it falls under trade and anything that is bought for the intention of selling and profiting from is zakatable. Any subsequent gains or losses will not be considered, only the net total remaining on the zakat anniversary date based on the market value of the stock.

- **Zakat on shares**: Zakat must be given on shares purchased for capital gain. It will be calculated according to the current market value. If shares are bought not for capital gain but to receive dividends from a company, then one pays zakat on one's share of the company one owns while subtracting the total value of non-zakatable items.

- **Zakat on dividends/cooperatives**: zakat must be paid on cash dividends which are corporate profits given to shareholders and so are governed by the rulings on general zakatable items.

- **Zakat and mortgages**: Generally, in the Hanafi School, long-term loans are not factored into the total zakatable liabilities. Only short-term loans are considered, i.e. those for immediate re-payments. Total mortgage payments therefore are not to be added. What is to be added is the total repayment figure of one lunar year.[79] **Example**: A bought house with a mortgage of £150,000 with £500 phm (per hijri month). It is not the total mortgage amount that is deducted from A's zakat liability (e.g. £150,000)

---

[79] Ibn ʾAbidin, *Radd al-Muhtar*, 2:260-261.

but the total repayment for one lunar year; in this case: £500 x 12 = £6000.

- **Zakat and student loans**: as a rule, zakat is always payable by the *creditor* (one in credit/owed the money) not the *debtor* (one in debt/who owes money). Any remaining amount of money of the student loan a person has is not subject to zakat. **Example**: A took out a student loan of £10,000 and deducted all expenses incurred during his university course (tuition fees, rent, etc.) and was left with £1000 at the end of the year. Zakat will not be applied on that because it is a debt. The reason why debt is not added to the zakat liability list – as the *fuqaha'* explain – is because freeing oneself from debt is a basic necessity in order to be protected from creditor action, harm or damage.

- **Zakat and pensions**: The basic reality of a pension is that citizen A pays automatic deductible contributions from earnings to the state over their working career and upon retirement of a certain age, the state returns that contribution back to A. **Example**, A pays National Insurance (NI) contribution of £30 every month for 25 years. The total amount of pension receivable would be £9000 upon retirement. <u>Zakat therefore is due on all voluntary pension schemes and not on those that were compulsorily deducted</u>. Until and unless a person actually has possession of the money, zakat will not be levied. There will also apply retrospective zakat liability, i.e. zakat will have to be given on all previous years as well.

- **Zakat on Stocks/shares**: Zakat must be given on stocks and shares that are purchased.[80] **Example**: If A buys shares in a company (i.e. the stocks of their business) as investment and receives dividends (profit) from it. Zakat will be subsequently levied on the dividends earned from the investment.

[End]

Praise be to Allah,
Abundant blessings on our beloved,
The Messenger of Allah,
His family and Companions
And all who follow them.

Completed in Rabi` al-Thani 1430 with the Help of Allah
Hampstead, London.
S. Z. Chowdhury

---

[80] That is, if one holds to buying and selling it being permitted.

KEY REFERENCES

Arabic References:

Ibn `Abidin, *Hashiyat Radd al-Muhtar `ala 'l-Durr al-Mukhtar Sharh Tanwir al-Absar*, 7 vols. Beirut: Dar al-Ihya' al-Turath al-`Arabi, n.d.

———— *Radd al-Muhtar `ala 'l-Durr al-Mukhtar*, 8 vols. Karachi: H. M. S. Co., 1986.

al-Bahlawi, *Adillat al-Hanafiyya min al-Ahadith al-Nabawiyya `ala 'l-Masa'il al-Fiqhiyya*, Damascus: Dar al-Qalam, 2007.

al-Maydani, *al-Lubab fi Sharh al-Kitab*, 4 vols. Karachi: Kutub Khana, n.d.

al-Haythami, *Majma` al-Zawa'id*, Cairo: Maktbat al-Qudsi, n.d.

———— al-Haythami, *Majma` al-Zawa'id*, Beirut: Dar al-Kitab al-`Arabi, 1982.

Ibn al-Humam, *Fath al-Qadir li 'l-`Ajiz al-Faqir Sharh al-Hidaya*, 9 vols. Beirut: Dar al-Ihya' al-Turath al-`Arabi, 1997.

al-Kasani, *al-Bada'i` al-Sana'i` fi Tartib al-Shara'i`*, 6 vols. Beirut: Dar al-Ihya' al-Turath al-`Arabi, 2000.

al-Marghinani, *al-Hidaya Sharh Bidyat al-Mubtadi*, 4 vols. Beirut: Dar al-Kutub al-`Ilmiyya, 2000.

Mawlana Nizam, et al. *al-Fatawa al-Hindiyya*, 6 vols. Quetta: Maktaba Majdiyya, 1983.

———— *al-Fatawa al-Hindiyya*, repr. Beirut: Dar al-Fikr, 1979.

———— *al-Fatawa al-Hindiyya*, 6 vols. Beirut: Dar Ihya' Turath al-`Arabi, 1980.

al-Mawsili, *Kitab al-Ikhtiyar li-Ta`lil al-Mukhtar*, 5 vols. Cairo: Dar al-Ma`rifa, 2000.

al-Nabhani, Taqi al-Din, *al-Shakhsiyya al-Islamiyya*, 3 vols. Beirut: Dar al-Umma, 2003-2005.

———— *Nizam al-Iqtisadi fi'l-Islam*, Beirut: Dar al-Umm, 2004.

al-Nadwi, S. al-*Fiqh al-Muyassar*, Karachi: Zam-Zam Publications, 2009.

Ibn Nujaym, *al-Bahr al-Ra'iq fi Sharh Kanz al-Daqa'iq*, 9 vols. Beirut: Dar al-Kutub al-`Ilmiyya, 1997.

al-Qal`aji, M. et al, *Mu`jam al-Lughat al-Fuqaha'*, Beirut: Dar al-Nafa'is, 2000.

al-Quduri, *al-Mukhtasar* (English-Arabic text, trans. M. Kiani, London: Dar al-Taqwa, 2009).

al-Shurunbulali, *Nur al-Idah* (English-Arabic text, trans. W. Charkawi) n.p. 2004.

————— *Maraqi al-Falah Sharh Nur al-Idah*, Damascus: Maktabat al-`Ilm al-Hadith, 2001.

————— *Maraqi al-Falah Sharh Nur al-Idah*, Beirut: Dar al-Kutub al-`Ilmiyya, 1995.

————— *Imdad al-Fattah Sharh Nur al-Idah*, Damascus, n.p. 2001.

————— *Maraqi al-Sa`adat*, Beirut: Dar al-Kutub al-Lubnani, 1973 and English trans. by F. A. Khan, London: Whitethread Press, 2010.

————— *Sabil al-Falah fi Sharh Nur al-Idah*, Beirut: Dar al-Bayruti, n.d.

Usmani, M. T. *Takmilat Fath al-Mulhim*, 3 vols. Karachi: Maktabat-i Dar al-`Ulum, 1986-1987.

Urdu References:

Khan, Ahmed Reza. *al-`Ataya li-Nabawiyya fi' l-Fatawa al-Ridwiyya*, 6 vols. Mubarakpur: Sunni Darul Isha'at, 1981.

————— *al-`Ataya al-Nabawiyya fi' l-Fatawa al-Ridwiyya*, 12 vols. Faisalabad: Maktaba Nuriyya Ridwiyya.

Ludhianvi, Rashid Ahmad. *Ahsan al-Fatawa*, Karachi: H. M. S. Co, 1398–.

Usmani, `Aziz al-Rahman. *`Aziz al-Fatawa*, Karachi: Darul Isha'at, n.d.

——————— `*Aziz al-Fatawa*, 2 vols. Deoband Fatwa Department, n.d.

www.ingramcontent.com/pod-product-compliance
Lightning Source LLC
Chambersburg PA
CBHW071643170526
45166CB00003B/1412